SEA LIONS

Colleen Stanley Bare

Illustrated with photographs by the author

A *Skylight* Book

DODD, MEAD & COMPANY

New York

To Jean

Library of Congress Cataloging-in-Publication Data

Bare, Colleen Stanley.
  Sea lions.

  (A Skylight book)
  Includes index.
  Summary: Text and photographs present the characteristics and hab-
its of the intelligent, curious, and playful sea lion.
  1. Sea lions—Juvenile literature. [1. Sea lions] I. Title.
QL737.P63B37 1986   599.74′6   85–16276
ISBN 0–396–08719–1

CONTENTS

Sea lions are sociable, playful animals.

1

The Playful Sea Lion

One misty morning on a rocky beach, several young male sea lions were together in shallow water near the shore. They were playing a game that could be called "get the sea lion off the rock." One of the animals was sitting on the top of a small boulder. The others kept shoving at him with their heads and necks until they finally pushed him off. Then another took his place, and the game began again.

Sea lions like to play. They frolic and chase each other through the ocean, twisting and making sharp turns with their shiny, black bodies. Sometimes they jump completely out of the water during their chases.

They are also expert body surfers and play games in some of the biggest waves. They often ride on the very crests of waves, inside them, or glide into shore directly ahead of them. Or they may leap back over the breakers just before the water crashes downward. Then they swim around, waiting for another one.

Sea lions frequently play with objects such as fish or seaweed. They toss them up into the air and then catch them in their mouths. They even play with other kinds of animals.

In the Galápagos Islands, six hundred miles off the coast of Ecuador in South America, there live some unusual reptiles called marine iguanas. These are large lizards that are two to four feet long, half of which is tail. They share the beaches and the surf with many sea lions. Unfortunately for the iguanas, the sea lions treat them like toys. They seem to delight in poking at the iguanas as they sit sunning on the rocks. When the reptiles try to escape by jumping into the water, the sea lions take after them, nipping and nudging. They also grab the iguanas' long tails and pull on them. The iguanas are not harmed during

Sea lions tease marine iguanas in the Galápagos Islands.

these chases but are certainly bothered and teased.

It is this fun-loving attitude and their excellent memories and ability to be trained that make sea lions particularly well suited for their roles as performers. They are often the acrobatic stars in water shows put on at zoos, circuses, and oceanariums all over the country. The clowning sea animal seen jumping through a hoop or balancing a ball on its nose at the amusement park is usually a well-trained sea lion.

Sea lions are attractive. Their whiskery faces and soft round eyes give them doglike appearances. They are amusing to watch on the beach because of their awkward movements.

A sea lion is able to walk efficiently on land, using all four of its webbed flippers as feet. But its head and neck swing from side to side as it waddles across

Sea lions have large eyes and sensitive whiskers.

A favorite sea lion pose.

the sand or rocks, making it look somewhat comical. Even more amazing is to watch a sea lion in a hurry, galloping across the ground at a rapid pace.

The sea lion often assumes an appealing pose that is usually a winner with humans. It will sit up straight with its short tail folded under the rounded body, head raised back, nose pointed in the air, often with the eyes closed. This gives the animal a gentle, wise, kindly appearance that can be very deceiving, especially during breeding time. Although sea lions have happy-go-lucky personalities, and are the most playful of all of the world's thirty-three members of the seal family, they are still wild animals.

2

Family Backgrounds

"Look at the seal," the girl cried to her classmates. She was on a school field trip to Point Lobos State Reserve at Carmel, California. "See, it's swimming around," she said, pointing to an animal in the surf below the cliff where the group was standing. "And there is another one, lying on a rock."

"Those are two different kinds of seals," said the teacher. "The one in the water is a sea lion, and the other on the rock is a true seal. They aren't the same."

The girl had made a common mistake, for many people think that all seals are alike. Actually, the swimmer she was watching was a California sea lion,

Sea lions live side by side with sea gulls, brown pelicans, and elephant seals.

Seal rocks at Point Lobos, Carmel, California.

one of the two kinds of sea lions in North America. The other kind is the Steller sea lion. Both often share the same territories and are found together on beaches and rocks at places like Point Lobos. The seal that the girl saw stretched out on the rock was a harbor seal, which is a member of a different family from the sea lions.

All seals and sea lions belong to a special scientific order called Pinnipedia, a Latin word meaning "fin-footed." Within this group are three families. One, called Otariidae, contains the "eared seals," which are the sea lions and the fur seals. They have small, inch-long ears. The second family, Phocidae, is made up of a number of "earless" seals, also called "true seals." They don't have outside ears and hear through a tiny round opening on each side of their heads. The third family, Odobenidae, consists of the walrus, which is also earless.

The eared seals and the walruses are able to travel on land much better than their true seal, earless cousins. This is because their large hind flippers can be turned forward under their bodies, allowing them to "walk" on all four fin-feet. The true seals have smaller flippers, and those in the rear cannot rotate. So they move across the beach on their bellies, using a wiggling, squirming motion. For this reason the sea lions, fur seals, and walruses are called the "walkers," and the true seals are the "crawlers."

Sea lions are so much at home in the sea that it is hard to believe they once were land animals. But scientists think that, until some 20 million years ago,

Sea lions have small, inch long ears.

Sea lions waddle when they walk.

they lived entirely on land. In fact, some say that they are related to the early bear. They probably originated in the North Pacific, near the seashore, and took to the ocean to find food. As they spent more and more time in the sea, their bodies gradually became streamlined and pointed, with their legs shortened and finlike. Over a period of millions of years, they became adapted to life in the water as well as on land.

There are five sea lion species in the world. The best known is the California sea lion (*Zalophus californianus*), because of its presence in most major zoos. It is also the popular "trained seal" of many circus and aquarium shows. It is found all along the Pacific Coast, from British Columbia to California and the coast of Mexico. Another group lives in the Galápagos Islands, off the coast of Ecuador in South America. A few that once lived in the Sea of Japan are now thought to have died out. Male California sea lions are up to eight feet long and can weigh as much as six hundred pounds. Females are much smaller, up to six feet and two hundred pounds. Males also have a distinctive bump or swelling on their heads, which doesn't appear until about age five years. They all have short brownish fur that looks shiny black when wet.

The northern sea lion (*Eumetopias jubatus*), also known as the Steller sea lion, is the only other species of sea lion in North America. It is found from the Bering Sea and the Aleutian Islands, along the coast of Alaska, and south to California. This is the species

Roaring sea lion bull. Note the bump on his head.

that, in 1741, was given the name "sea lion" by the famous explorer-naturalist Georg Wilhelm Steller, because of its lionlike roar and the bull's shaggy mane. The Steller sea lion is much larger than the California sea lion. The males are up to eleven feet in length and weigh as much as two thousand pounds, with the females up to seven feet and six hundred pounds.

When wet, the coat becomes smooth, shiny, and dark.

Group of California sea lions hauled out on the rocks.

The Steller's coat is tan, and the animal is generally quieter than the noisy California sea lion.

The South American sea lion (*Otaria byronia*) lives along the coasts of South America and the Falkland Islands. It is large, with the males up to eight feet and twelve hundred pounds and females six feet and three hundred pounds. Only slightly smaller are the other two sea lion species, both found in the regions of Australia and New Zealand. These are the Austra-

Steller sea lions are very large.

lian sea lion (*Neophoca cinerea*) and the New Zealand or Hooker's sea lion (*Neophoca hookeri*).

All sea lions have much in common. The males are called *bulls*, the females *cows*, and the babies are *pups*. They breathe air and are mammals, which means that they are warm-blooded and the females produce milk for their young. They also mate and give birth to their young on land. But about three-fourths of their lives is spent in the ocean.

3

Swimming and Diving

People who have gone swimming with sea lions say that it is a lot of fun. The animals are curious and will put their whiskery noses right up to human faces. Visitors to the Galápagos Islands, who are warned not to touch any of the wildlife, are told that they may not kiss the sea lions. However, it is all right for the sea lions to kiss them. Which is exactly what they seem to do, swimming among the tourists in the surf. But no human could ever keep up with these skillful swimmers and divers.

Sea lions swim with grace and beauty, at speeds up to twenty miles an hour. Their torpedo-shaped

bodies almost seem to "fly" through the sea. They use their long foreflippers like oars or paddles to make swift downward strokes. The hind flippers serve as rudders and do the steering. Each of the four fins is webbed and has five "toes" or "fingers." Sea lions frequently "porpoise" as they swim, meaning that they leap out of the water, with their bodies curved, and reenter headfirst. Groups are sometimes seen swimming in single file, porpoising one after another as they travel.

The famous ocean explorer Jacques Cousteau and his diving team kept two male sea lions aboard their ship *Calypso* for several months, to study them. The human divers swam and dived with the sea lions, which they named Pepito and Cristobald. They reported that the animals appeared happiest when they were in the water, cavorting around the human divers. The sea lions shot up toward the surface like rockets and then went spinning down to the bottom.

But even using diving equipment, the men could not go down as deep in the ocean as the sea lions. This is because sea lions are able to dive to a depth

Sea lions are curious.

Sea lions are expert swimmers.

of more than twelve hundred feet, considerably deeper than the Cousteau group had ever been able to explore. The animals can stay underneath the water for up to twenty minutes before they have to come back up for a breath. During a dive, their bodily processes are slowed down and oxygen is directed to the hearts and the brains. Humans cannot do this and must breathe through special oxygen tanks to stay underwater. They also have to come back to the surface in stages, or they will get a dangerous, sometimes fatal, illness called the "bends." Sea lions have none of these problems and can dive deep into the sea and shoot back up to the surface without any ill effects.

The United States Navy has made use of the diving skills of sea lions in a program called "Operation Quick Find." The animals are taught to recover torpedoes and missiles from the bottoms of the oceans. Their superior memories and ability to learn commands make them especially suitable for such missions.

Sea lions have a special blanket to keep them warm in the chilly waters. This is a thick layer of fat under the skin, called blubber. Therefore, the cold does not seem to bother them and they can stay in the ocean indefinitely. They are even able to sleep in the sea, instinctively rising to the surface to take a breath

Sea lions floating offshore with their flippers sticking out of the water.

about every twenty minutes. Along the Pacific Coast it is not unusual to see groups of sea lions sleeping in the water just offshore. Their back flippers often stick up out of the water as they float.

There is one very important reason for the sea lions spending so much time in the ocean. It is their fish market. They are carnivores, or meat eaters, and hunt for their food in the sea. Their meat is fish and includes squid, octopus, abalone, and other varieties. They consume fifteen to twenty pounds of fish a day. However, because of their stores of fat, they are able to go for several weeks without eating if necessary.

Sea lions also have a strange habit of eating pebbles and stones. When scientists examined the stomach contents of some of the animals, they found rocks as large as hens' eggs and tennis balls. Stones weighing as much as twenty-four pounds were discovered in one stomach. The reason for this remains a mystery. Some say that the stones help to grind up food. Or perhaps they provide extra weight for balancing in the water. Or do they keep the animals from becoming so hungry between feedings? No one really knows.

Sea lion senses help them to find fish in the sea. They have large eyes with pupils that are able to expand in the water so that they can see, even in the dimmest light. Although their ears and nostrils close up underwater, they are able to sense movement from nearby fish. But it is their whiskers that are probably the most helpful in fishing. Long and stiff, they have nerve endings that make them very sensitive. When a sea lion's whiskers touch a fish, the animal grabs it with sharp, pointed teeth. Even blind sea lions are able to find food in this way. The sense of touch

Sea lions have large eyes. Their eyes lack tear ducts, so they often look as though they are crying.

through the whiskers also helps in avoiding sharp rocks at the bottom of the sea.

Although sea lions are at home in the sea, they also must spend many weeks on land.

4

Pupping Time
on the Beach

It is pupping time on the sandy beach of a remote
island, and there is bedlam. The month is June, and
thousands of sea lions have returned from the sea
to the place where they were born. They have come
to give birth to their young and to mate. The beach
is jammed, and the noise is deafening. Sea lions bark,
bellow, roar, and scream all day and all night. Bulls
battle and pups are born, all part of the ritual that
happens every year at sea lion rookeries.

Sea lion breeding grounds are called rookeries. In
the spring, the bulls return to the rookeries after
spending many months in the ocean. West Coast Stel-

California sea lions are noisy.

Adults and juveniles on the rocks.

ler and California sea lion males often migrate as far
north as British Columbia and must travel long dis-
tances to get back to their home rookeries. As soon
as they arrive, the battles begin. The bulls stake out
favorite territories, or breeding areas, on the beach.
They then must defend these territories by fighting

off other bulls. They bite, slash with their teeth, shove and push. The winners are the most aggressive, strongest, and usually the largest bulls. They become the beachmasters or lords of their territories. The losers stay together in bachelor groups, outside of the territories. They engage in mock battles with each other, and some wait for a chance to sneak back and challenge the beachmasters.

Soon the females arrive and gather in groups within the beachmasters' territories. These groups are called

Fighting on the rocks.

harems and usually have from ten to twenty cows. Shortly after the females' arrival, each cow gives birth to a single pup. Then she mates with a beachmaster, which will result in the birth of another pup in about a year. Meanwhile, the beachmasters continue to defend their harems and territories. They patrol up and down the beach and through the surf, barking constantly. By the end of the breeding season, sea lion bulls are exhausted and hoarse.

Scientists have studied sea lions on beaches in the Galápagos Islands and in the Channel Islands off the coast of Southern California. They say that the animals are just as active at night as during the day. Roaring beachmasters fight off challengers, cows noisily quarrel with each other, and pups play and bleat for their mothers. Researchers who have lived in tents among the sea lions report many sleepless nights.

Sea lion pups come into the world fully furred and with their eyes open. They can move around and walk on their flippers within thirty minutes. California sea lion babies weigh twelve to fourteen pounds at birth and are about thirty inches long. Steller pups are

A pup just born on a beach in the Galápagos Islands.

larger, around three feet in length and weighing thirty pounds.

As soon as a pup is born, the mother nuzzles and smells it so that she can recognize its particular odor. The pup also begins to "talk" with its mother. She repeats a honking call over and over, and the pup answers with a lamblike bleat. This communication is very important to the pup's survival. In about four days the mother will begin to leave the pup and go out into the sea to find food. When she returns, she

A cow calling her pup.

will give her distinctive call, and the pup will answer.
This is how they will get back together, amid the
thousands of barking, roaring sea lions and their bleating pups. When the mother finds her baby, she smells
it to further identify it. Then she nurses the hungry
infant. She will only nurse her own pup, and if another tries to sneak a meal, she may pick it up in

40

her mouth and toss it as far as fifteen feet. Sea lion milk is very rich, about 37 percent fat, and pups grow very rapidly. California sea lion pups are nursed for about six months, whereas Steller pups nurse for a year or more. However, they all are able to digest small fish within a few months after birth.

Sea lion mothers are very protective of their young and refuse to leave them for the first few days after

A sea lion mother will only nurse her own pup.

A close-up of a two-week-old sea lion pup.

birth. If she senses danger, a cow will move her pup
to a safer location. She will pick it up by the nape
of its neck, catlike, and drag it across sand, rocks,
and even into the water. On sunny days, she may
have to make repeated trips to tide pools to get wet

42

and keep her insulated body from becoming over-heated. If her pup is under a week old, she will take it along, often struggling and bleating, and drag it into the water with her. She will also try to protect the pup from being crushed by a bull. Aggressive beachmasters charge down the beach to drive out intruders, running over anything in their way, including pups.

By the time the pups are two weeks old, the mothers regularly leave them to go fishing in the sea. Sometimes they are gone for two to three days. Now the pups begin to gather together in pup groups.

5

The Pup Groups

Sea lion pups look somewhat like dog puppies with fins. At first the flippers seem too big for their bodies, and their skin has deep folds. But they grow very quickly.

After the first few days, their mothers spend time fishing at sea. And the pups start wandering around the rookery. They join with other pups in groups, sometimes called *pup pods*, which may contain as few as five or as many as two hundred. Now their days are devoted to learning how to swim in shallow water at the edge of the sea, sleeping on the beach, and playing.

Sea lion pups look like dog puppies with fins.

Pups are very sociable and constantly play. They nip and shove at each other and scuffle on the ground. They play games that could be called "toss the seaweed," "throw the fish," and "follow the leader." They push at one another with their necks and play-fight like the adults, all good training for future battles. They chase each other through the water, leaping

45

A two-week-old pup swimming.

and splashing, and blow bubbles through their noses. Their frolicking gives them practice in swimming and diving. But when their mothers return from the sea, their games cease and they are ready for meals of warm milk.

Like all babies, sea lion pups sleep a lot. They lie stretched out on the beach, often with their mothers. But frequently they sleep in tightly packed pup pods, using each other for pillows. They adopt the same sleeping positions as the adults. Sometimes they sleep on their bellies with all four flippers folded underneath. Or they lie on their sides, foreflippers against their bodies and the hind ones extended out to the

Pups play follow the leader.

rear. They even sleep sitting up on their front fins with the heads thrown back.

Sea lions spend a lot of time grooming themselves. Pups start grooming at an early age, in the same way as their elders. Using the nail-like claws on the hind flippers, they can scratch almost all parts of their bodies. They groom their fur with the foreflippers and

This pup is still nursing, even though it is almost as large as its mother.

sometimes roll on their backs and scrape against rocks. Their whiskers get cleaned by being rubbed against smooth stones or other sea lions, first on one side of the snouts and then the other.

As the pups grow older, they gradually move from the tide pools into deeper sea channels, to play and learn to fish. By the time they are weaned, they are ready to go to sea with their mothers. Little is known about the migrating habits of sea lions. However, scientists do say that the bulls leave the rookeries first, often traveling hundreds of miles in coastal waters. The cows and their pups follow in a few months but stay in the vicinity of the rookeries.

6

A Dangerous World

One bright September morning a group of sea lions was sunning on the rocks and swimming in shallow waters off the coast of Monterey, California. Suddenly, without warning, they were attacked. The attackers came into the shore, their huge black fins swiftly cutting through the water. They were killer whales out looking for a meal. In an instant, they grabbed some of the sea lions in their huge jaws, while the rest of the animals fled in fright. It was all over very quickly.

Killer whales and sharks are the sea lions' major natural predators. Playful young sea lions are especially in danger. In the Galápagos Islands, hammer-head sharks are common predators.

Bad weather is another serious threat to sea lion survival. The animals are battered against rocks and cliffs during storms. Pups are often washed off rocks and swept into the sea before they have learned to swim.

A recent event called El Niño was very damaging to many of the sea lions on the West Coast and in the Galápagos Islands. The term means "Christ child." El Niño was originally named by Peruvian fishermen because it happens around Christmastime along the coast of South America. Now it is used to

Killer whale.

Sea lions are found along the rocky coast. They are sometimes battered against the rocks during storms.

describe the abnormal warming of the seas that occurs every few years off the coasts of both North and South America. El Niño struck again beginning in 1982, and its effects will be felt for many years. One-third of the Pacific Ocean, from southern Chile to the Gulf of Alaska, was affected. Water temperatures were up to five degrees above normal along the Pacific Coast and fourteen degrees along the west coast of South America. This caused the destruction of kelp beds and forage at the bottom of the sea, resulting in great change in the marine life. Fish were unable to find food and either starved or moved away. And marine mammals, such as sea lions, which normally feed on the fish, went hungry.

The most serious effects of El Niño were felt in 1983. The carcasses of young sea lions began to wash up on beaches along the Pacific Coast. And at the rookeries, there was a dying-off of pups. When the mothers went to sea to feed, they had to go farther and farther away from the shore to find any fish. Many of them never returned to nurse their young, and the pups starved to death. The year 1983 was a disastrous one for baby sea lions in the Galápagos Islands, and practically all of the pups were lost, due to El Niño.

El Niño also caused changes in atmospheric pressure that allowed storm after storm to batter the Pacific Coast. Sea lions were washed away as land fell into the sea, and many of the young were drowned during weeks of drenching rains and high seas. To everyone's relief, El Niño departed in 1984.

Sea lions suffer from diseases. In 1970, large numbers of California sea lions died from a bacterial infection called leptospirosis. Another serious epidemic of leptospirosis was reported in 1984–1985, again affecting the West Coast California sea lion population. The disease causes damage to the animals' kidneys and livers and is often fatal unless treated with antibiotics. In the early 1970s, more than half of the population of Galápagos sea lions was killed by an encephalitis-like disease. Sea lions can get pneumonias and are afflicted with parasites such as mites, lice, and worms.

But the sea lion's major enemy is man. The killing of sea lions for commercial purposes began in the seventeenth century. Considered valuable for their skins and blubber, both California and Steller sea lions were ruthlessly slaughtered. Even into this century, sea lions were killed for dog food. Finally, in 1972, the Marine Mammal Protection Act was passed by

A sick young sea lion at the California Marine Mammal Center.

the United States Congress. This forbids the killing or capturing of any marine mammals except by special permission. In California, permits are issued by the Department of Fish and Game for the capture of live sea lions for the purposes of exhibition and research. About a hundred such permits are issued each year.

The sea lions' conflicts with man have not ended. They eat fish, making them enemies of many fishermen. Consequently, some illegal killings of the mammals have been reported. Another man-made problem occurs because of the animal's habit of scavenging and man's habit of littering. Sea lions will swallow all kinds of hard objects such as bottle caps, plastic bags and toys, can-top rings, knives, and even rubber balls. Such items, left on beaches and swept out to sea, or given to the animals in zoos, can damage their stomachs. Sea lions also become entangled in fishing nets and starve to death.

But although man is the sea lion's major enemy, he can also be a good friend.

7

Man As a Friend

She was a huge, blind Steller sea lion found stranded on a Pacific Coast beach near the Oregon border. By the time the rescue team from the California Marine Mammal Center arrived to pick her up, she was very sick. They caged her, with difficulty, and she was taken by truck to the Center, located across the Bay from San Francisco. There, the trained staff worked around the clock to try to save her. They treated her with injections of antibiotics, steroids, and vitamin B complex. She also had to be force-fed until she was able and willing to eat on her own.

This is a familiar story to the hundreds of volunteers who work to protect and save marine mammals.

The Marine Mammal Center was organized to rescue, treat, and study sea mammals found stranded along the Pacific Coast. The animals are usually sick, injured, or simply too weak to swim. The Center covers fourteen coastal counties in Northern California. Its goal is to return healthy, wild marine animals to the sea. Other rescue operations are conducted by Sea World in San Diego and the Marine Mammal Center in Santa Barbara. Research is an important part of these programs, and scientists and veterinarians study the animals to learn more about them.

Sometimes a rescued sea lion doesn't seem to want to go back to its former home in the ocean, such as one called Nelson. After being rehabilitated at the California Marine Mammal Center, he was taken out to sea and released. It was hoped that he would be able to lead the life of a normal sea lion bull. Instead, he returned to the vicinity of the Center three different times, once showing up at a nearby college. Finally, it was decided that he was unable to fend for himself. The Center shipped him to Ocean World, an oceanarium at Fort Lauderdale, Florida. Soon word came back of Nelson's latest escapade. One morning he was missing from his pool. After a frantic search, it was discovered that he had scaled a six-foot fence, landing in the next pool. There he was found swimming with more than fifty sharks, after having eaten a live barracuda.

Some animals cannot be released, because of adjustment problems or serious ailments. These are often placed in zoos or aquariums around the country.

Humans who work with sea lions frequently become their friends. Jacques Cousteau and his diving team found that the two sea lions, Pepito and Cristobald, liked to be petted and stroked.

Sea lions are often the stars of shows put on at zoos and oceanariums. Their performances look effortless. But it really takes great patience to train a sea lion to do tricks such as balancing a ball on its nose or jumping through a hoop. First the trainer must make friends with the animal. Then the trick is taught by using the voice, rewards of food, and displays of affection like petting and gentle scratching. For example, ball balancing is taught by repeatedly putting a ball on the sea lion's nose until it accidentally balances. Immediately the trainer praises the ani-

Trained sea lion "playing" basketball.

mal and gives it some fish, which reinforces the desired action. Soon the sea lion will learn to balance the ball on command. The trick of "rolling over" is presented in the same way as for a dog. The trainer pats the animal, gently grasping the flippers, and nudges it over. As it rolls over, the command "over" is given, with the reward of fish. Similar techniques are used to teach routines like playing basketball, diving from a platform, and doing flipper-walks. A real crowd pleaser is having a child come forward to receive a whiskery sea lion kiss, which is really just a gentle shove against the cheek. The animals seem to delight in doing tricks, and they respond to the applause of their appreciative audiences. But most of all, they like the rewards of fish and praise.

Sea lions can live a long time when they are cared for and protected by man. Their life-span in the wild is usually from five to fifteen years, whereas in captivity they may last for more than twenty.

These are magnificent animals. They are intelligent, curious, playful, and a joy to watch. Both man and sea lion have much to gain by being good friends.

Index